Bro. Germany

7/1/07

Jesus Muhammad Ali

The Evolution of the Nation of Islam

THE STORY OF THE
HONORABLE ELIJAH MUHAMMAD

The
Evolution of
the Nation of Islam

THE STORY OF THE
HONORABLE ELIJAH MUHAMMAD

Jesus Muhammad-Ali

GRANDSON

JMA
Publishing

Library of Congress Catalog Number:PAu-2-322-085

ISBN: 0-9725192-0-3

Printed in the United States

Dedicated to the memory of my
beloved Grandfather,

The Honorable Elijah Muhammad
(May Allah Grant him with the Mercy and Bless him
with Paradise)

Contributors include:

Great Grandmother "Mother Marie" Muhammad,
The Honorable Elijah Muhammad, Sis. Clara Muhammad,
Aunt Lottie (Ryah), Uncle Jam Muhammad, Aunt Berrnastine,
Sheik Muhammad Almana, Min. James Shabazz,
Bro. Murad Muhammad

In loving memory of my wife,

Mrs. Loraz R. Lewis Muhammad-Ali

CONTENTS

———————

PREFACE

Born and Raised Under the Wing

As a child who witnessed the level of humility shown him by my parents and by the thousands who followed him, then, as a young man who grew to feel privileged to find myself in his company, this was the Honorable Elijah Muhammad (May Allah Grant him the Mercy), the man who I called grandpa. If it was standing security at his side, unflinching for hours as he delivered a Sunday lecture or spending 16 plus hours a day, as his personal aid and valet or internal security and trusted confidant, whatever the title of my duties, 'son' was his most common reference. If it was standing before thousands at one of the National Conventions, in his Hyde Park Palace, or on his private jet bound for one the lavishly appointed villas of Mexico, I always felt quite blessed to be in his presence. However, in those last few weeks, my duties came to be represented as his doctor's intermediary for the family, after he'd fallen into comma at Chicago's Mercy Hospital.

The reader should be made aware this book is presented in my voice and has not been grammatically embellished, for a number of heartfelt reasons. In this regard, I ask your indulgence. However, the material written from a national and oftentimes international overview, while communicated in a way or jargon dialect if you will, my family and I, have found effective when communicating the message to the grass roots, the deep seated passions identified in the heart wrenching self destructive psychological cancer that has taken root, particularly among our young, and predominately based in our inner city minority communities.

ONE

Background:

*a) The Holy Quran,
"Allah is the knower of the Unseen" and
the perceptive impact posed by this concept,
born out of the Industrial Revolution.*

Islam and so its Umah (body of believers) struggle with as-signing conceptual placement for the repetitively stated Quranic phrase or reference: "Allah is the Knower of the Unseen!" Place-ment of this concept is found to be most confounding, ever since the dawn of the Industrial Revolution," and marking the fall of the Turkish Ottoman Empire and the Islamic Khilafah State. The impact and Cultural shock faced by Arabia, an ancient culture bound mind, body, and soul by Quranic edicts, then suddenly finding itself caught-up in a world in which things are moving about without touch or beast of burden. The Islamic scholars and clergy, labor with indexing or giving broad-based placement to this concept. Although, an imposed interpretation as to those given power over "The Unseen" force of energy as ascribed to the Caucasian west: this is a statement defined as **"Allah's Befriendment"** (*often misinterpreted to have racial connotations, as to white supremacy*). The Holy Quran, interpreted to mean: (The Book of sprirtual healing) "for those who seek guidance". A book written in the first person or God's Voice, chapter or Sura means word picture and "Allah is the Giver of the word". Written in a format that's quite unlike the Holy Bible and Gospel, this Book, in broad generalities identifies the various charater traits of the human spirit (for our evaluation of self and others).

Aside from the powerful economic inducement, the profound impact of this concept invoked by this phrase, concluding the West having won Allah's befriendment, coupled with Arabia's embrace of America's 28th President Woodrow Wilson's idealism after World War I, laying way for establishment of an East-West alliance that **placed an Ocean of Oil (cheap energy) at the disposal of America at the dawn of the Industrial Revolution.** Energy and its multitude of applications, brought to market at a cost found to be cheaper than drilling domestically (1968 Saudi crude went for $2.25 per barrel or less than water). In the words of Sheik Mohammad Almama: " No water pressure, just push a hole in the sand and the black crude leaps up."

Master W. D. Fard Muhammad

TWO

Background:

b) Master Fard Muhammad, A product of the fall of the Ottoman Empire! Khilafah Islamic State

The aftermath of World War I and the fall of the Ottoman Empire gave rise to America's new-found philosophy of the Honorable Elijah Muhammad's "Nation of Islam" (May Allah Grant him the Mercy and Bless him with the Paradise), a philosophy as espoused by Elijah Muhammad's Arabian born mentor and teacher, known as and introducing himself as Master Wallace D. Fard Muhammad (born: February 26, 1877). It was this Arab, who was the Social and Philosophical architect of the "Jacob's Ladder"- like approach that gripped the hearts and minds of America's disenfranchised and often Institutionally discarded (the powerful potential found in people with nothing to lose). Master Fard Muhammad arrived in America's industrial capital of Detroit, Michigan, on July 4, 1930, to proclaim the birth of "The Nation of Islam."

A graduate of UCLA, Maser Fard Muhammad, was a man well aquainted with America's Constitutional protections, as provided by "the separation of Church and State," the seeds of this new-found religious-based Movement quickly took root in communities of America's disenfranchised, downtrodden Blacks, or so-called Negroes. A people up from chattel slavery, were quite receptive to phrases like "Up You Mighty Race, You Can Accomplish What You Will!" America's creed or idealism was merely a comic book fantasy met with no fanfare from the Black so called Negro communities of the 1930's, faced with overt psychological and socio-economic oppressive conditions that were not brought to challange, only until confronted by the racially charged era of America's Civil Rights Movement.

However, in the 1930's, with phrases of brazen condemnation like "The White Man is the Devil" (or racially speaking our devil). "The Hate which produced the Hate!" A statement asking White America to look in the mirror as it applies to the treatment of her former chattel.

Dr. King in Washington, D. C.

The Honorable Elijah Muhammad with Dr. King

THREE

Background:

c) Islam's Global Impact upon the super powers, the fall of Soviet Union and now, 9-11

On Independence Day July 4, 1930, as the Saudi Royal family signed to form the Saudi/American trade allaince of Aramco, America found herself in the grips of the Great Depression, Professor Wallace D. Fard Muhammad arrived in this country to proclaim his ministry. Professor Wallace D. Fard Muhammad aka Master Fard Muhammad, whose stated birthplace was just outside of Arabia's Holy City of Mecca, the son of Alfonso, a wealthy cloth merchant. W. D. Fard Muhammad, raised in Mecca under the Ottoman Turkish "Khalifah rule." The Khalif State was guardian to Islam's three Sacred Precincts of Mecca, Jerusalem and Medina (see appendix photos). In 1923, at the fall of the Ottoman Empire, Master Fard had reached 46 years of age and therefore, well inculcated, as it applies to the ideas and theology of the Islamic State.

The rule passed down from the Khalif (Caliph), whose power in the Islamic world was much like that of the Pope in Roman

The Holy City of Mecca, The performance of the Hajj

Catholicism. This meant that millions of Muslims (African and Arab alike) in arms answered to the Khalifah Rule, acting as Allah's "Vicegerent" charged with interpreting and seeing to the execution of the laws and edicts as revealed by Prophet Muhammad (May the Peace and Blessing of Allah be upon him). This reverence and complete devotion is symbolized by "Khaba," in the Holy City of Mecca; the first temple built to the worship of the "One God" by the Holy Prophets—Abraham and his two sons, Isaac and Ishmael (May Allah be Pleased with them). The Arab bloodline is traced by way of the Holy Prophet Ishmael; one of their sacred duties was to preserve this history. Master Fard Muhammad was said to have been found worthy to read thousands of years of said recordings, alleged to have been destroyed by the Ottoman Turks in or approximately the year 1918, before permitting such a reverent history to fall into the hands of those who had allied themselves with barbarous unbelievers. Barbarians who in conquest had come to murdered even members of prophet Muhammad (SWAS) family (May Allah be Please with them).

As a prelude to the World War I, a Jihad (Holy War) against all non-Muslims was declared by the Ottoman Turkish Khilafa State in 1914, during which more than a million Armenians were brutally slaughtered as town after town was ravaged. A petition from the Armenians against the present Turkish government, now pending before the United Nations, dates back to this event. The ramifications included the ultimate alignment in World War I. This particular slaughter in the name of religion lent further strength to the establishment of the Soviet Union as an antireligious state, aided by the later machinations of the "mad monk," the seven-foot religious zealot, Rasputin.

The aforementioned blood-stained page in the history of the Khalafa state continues to haunt Islam today, as the demise of the USSR in the Balkans, they deliberately left an imbalance along ethnic lines, when it came to murdered tens of thousands of

Thomas E. Lawrence / Lawrence of Arabia

Muslims, in what was genericly termed an ethnic cleansing (May Allah Grant them with the Mercy). One could only speculate as to why the former Soviet Union would leave such a horrific imbalance of power between such embittered ethnic rivals, could it have been a backhand slap in departure, at Islam? After all, the USSR's collapse came shortly after a most unpopular War in Afghanistan, that morally ripped the Soviet people apart, like the Vietnam War did America. 34% of the Soviet military was made-up of compromised ambivalent Muslim, often found giving the Soviet arms to their Afghani Muslim brothers, while they found the Saudi's closing ranks against there suffering economy when they stopped spending $6 billion (USD) annually, in American oil money for Soviet arms.

Imam Abdul Azziz Al Saud fought on horseback in armed combat with the Turks to establish himself as Arabia's first king, over Islam's Holy Land. However, the Arabic word which has been translated as king (Malik) means "owner," and Allah in the Holy Quran makes it quite clear, only He Owns us. A description of this page of history can be found in the the the exploits and sagas of the British soldier and scholar, Thomas E. Lawrence, the renowned "Lawrence of Arabia." **The foundation for the fall of the Khalifah Rule was laid down in a tabled debate on the floor of the Khalifah's Islamic Council.** This is Arabia, just after the turn of the century and World War I, rigidly molded by an ancient culture, as the religious edicts of the Khalifah Rule index-ing every aspect of the faithful's daily life. However, the Islamic Council was faced with the question "How can a forty-ton train be moved down a track without beast of burden?" The implied reference of this question speaks to a Quranic context, as it applies to those who were granted power over **"The Unseen."** The fol-lowing assertion goes unchallenged to date: "This is a statement of Allah's Befriendment; how can we not befriend one who Allah has Befriended?" The end result, this and its Quranic contextual inference, left unchallenged, laid the foundation on the Council floor of the Khalifah Islamic State, for the establishment of what would become a Saudi-Western alliance of Aramco Oil Corporation! *Leveraging this Quranic concept would constitute a door of opportunity left open, for the trade allaince, by, Allah's Frequently Used verse of the Holy Quran: "Allah is the Knower of the Unseen."* By the end of the 1930's, as the world became engulfed by World War II, the stench of their deep-seated hatreds subsequently left the door of the Arab world open to the migrating European Jewish people with Hitler's ruthless scourge at their back, when coming to gage their prospects for settlement in the Holy Land, they came to coin the phrase : *"The Arabs hate one another more than they could hate anyone (else)!"* Yes, often those who are viewed as brothers in the faith,as Muslims (by our own hand, destroy ourselves), belonging to a religion that states, after confessing our belief in the One God and His Messenger, its simply, "our prayers go for naught, less it be by our deeds!". It is upon our good deeds that rest acceptance, **by the Mercy**; of the offering of the 5 pillars of faith, to include prayer, fasting, charity, and making Hajj. An edict made clear in the Hadith: *"For Prophet Muhammad (SAAW) was sent down to complete the good manners"*. While from this we understand those who are sent down, so do they return to their Lord, as their ways are found to be in evidence.

The Jewish people learned one thing from Nazi Germany, if nothing else, man is the judge of his affairs, while He, Who is the Lord of all the Worlds, He is the Ultimate Judge of us all! Even though secularism was rejected by the Holy Prophet Muhammad (May the Peace and Blessing of Allah be upon him), the stench of the Arab blood feuds date back to the bloodletting expansionistic exploits of the Companions of Prophet Muhammad (SAAW), when one of the Companions, named Mouwi, an Imam and General of one of their huge armies executed Hussain the grandson of the Prophet, and son of Ali, (May Allah grant him with the Mercy) and the 3rd Kalif (May Allah grant him with the Mercy and the Paradise). In Mouwi's view, Hussain permitted the believers to worship his person: They were known to have come from miles around, just to touch Hussain, when Prophet Muhammed (SAAW) clearly stated: "I'm not establishing my family as an aristocracy", with a bloodline statement as to their birthright of privilege (a Hadith, in no doubt was taken as a mandate).

Jerusalem's Al Aqsa Mosque / "Dome of the Rock"

Four

Background:

d) Arab Tribal Rivalry,
Dating back to the slaughter of Hussein,
the grandson of Prophet Muhammad,
(May Allah be pleased with him).

The conquest of the mainly Wahhabi Sunni fundamentalist sect under Imam Abdul Azziz Al Saud formed the Saudi Royal Throne, as a 50 / 50 shared power between the Royal family and the Islamic Council (established to govern under Sharia Law, as governed by the Word of Allah, as revealed by the Holy Quran). The sovereignty of the Arabian monarch was in great part secured, after America's Standard Oil Company's excavation proposal and the subsequent events, i.e., providing funding that bolstered their military campaigns: $8 million in gold, non-refundable, for exclusive excavation rights, neighboring Kuwait having already made a huge find. The contract stated that in the event oil was discovered, profits must be shared equally with Standard Oil and the Royal Family as a birthright property.

Many Saudis in government have come to romantically embrace America and her place of world prominence as her sponsoring ally, reflecting upon her world station. Prior to the advent of their Saudi-American Oil Company, Aramco, in 1930, the Saudi's thought (respectfully in the Sheikh's words): "America was just some place off in the wilderness." The Saudi's with an ocean of oil at the dawn of the Industrial Revolution; "Just push a hole in the sand and the oil just leaps out of the ground". The Saudi Sheiks find themselves at difference with the Royal Family, who bank their oil proceeds with US Federal Reserve, drawing down only the 4% interest and creating a schism in the Government: *Since the days of the Ayyatollah, guarded by 100,000 Pakistani "Royal Guards", their banking policy is characterized as a reflection of the Royal Family's lack of trust in their own subjects or citizens.* While the Saudi Royal family fails to back its own currency, a government faced with hundreds of billions in debt as thousands, of Wahhabi Sheiks forming their Islamic Council or what was fashioned to be 50% of the Saudi Throne, in light of the Saudi Royal family's level of support of American interest, since 1930. America, a nation who adopted the Zionist Welfare State in 1948, as a client State, when today CNN and Al Jazeera, Qatar an Arabian Gulf sponsored broadcast, provides a 24 / 7 coverage of heart wrenching satellite programming of the Zionist occupation of Jerusalem's Holy Land territories of Palestine, while at the end of President Clinton's term in office America had spent 100 billion dollars seeking to broker a lasting peace in the area. A matter that reached an urgent level of address of global concern, on September 11, 2001 (9-11), when 15 of the 19 hijackers were identified as Saudi nationals. It brought America and so the World, a different nature of treacherous behavior to deal with.

"Sight of Heavenly Peace" a commemorative portrait framing President Carter's role in the landmark Camp David Accords.

FIVE

The Un-Godly Betrayal:

"And hold fast, all together, by the Rope which Allah, stretches out for you, and be not divided among yourselves; for ye were enemies and He joined your hearts in love, so that by His Grace, ye became brethren; and ye were on the brink of the Pit of Fire, and He saved you from it. Thus doth Allah Make His Signs clear to you; that ye may be guided."

The Holy Quran (Chapter) S.3 (Verse) A.103

In 1948 the sovereignty of the Jewish State was proclaimed in the name of Israel, which meant, in Arabic as in Hebrew, "the chosen or favored by God" (as it is written in the Holy Quran). America declared the Jewish State its "Client State," while supporting its right to secure its borders with nuclear arms. Despite this stance, the oil never stopped flowing. This was no less questioned than the Saudis spending their $8 billions fueling the economy of the Soviet Union for arms. This Saudi-American relationship endured in the spirit of, "You help my enemy and I shall be obliged to help yours." This held up until the seventies, when the Saudi Oil interruption and the Yom Kippur War, the advent of the OPEC cartel and the $30-plus-a-barrel oil prices changed the political scene. The Soviet arms relationship dissolved and not very long afterward, the

**The Former World Trade Center, a Cornerstone
of Capitalism and the Free World interest**

Dreams and lives shattered, when the worlds of East and West collide.

Soviet Union did likewise. While the Saudi Royals were pondering what color Rolls Royce to buy or whether their new palaces might be lavishly refurbished, three wars–1948, 1967 and 1973–meant death had surely touched every Egyptian home. It appears that since the signing of the Camp David Accord, the Saudis or the "Arab World" have been unable to find another mercenary army or group of paradise seekers to feed to America's lion on a leash (Israel). When you let other people define God's word, establishing for you their own yardstick of interpretation, you make them your intercessor. The Saudis had been keepers of the faith and custodians of Islam's most sacred precincts of Mecca and Medina. However, the Royal family's allied sponsorship of America had everything to do with the deep seated secular fears they have of one another, Now, America has spent a $100 billion seeking to address their Jewish State's assimilation problem with her 700 million Arab Muslim neighbors.

The aforementioned disclosure is provided as a historical preface, framed in a time-related sequence, to afford an evolutionary insight as to the make-up and character of one, Professor Wallace D. Fard Muhammad or Master W.D. Fard Muhammad, teacher and mentor of my grandfather, founder of the Nation of Islam as an organization, proclaimed under its national banner with the red sun background, crescent moon and five-pointed star. The flag has the likeness of the Turkish flag; only the crescent moon was turned, obviously, because they are Caucasian Muslims.

There have been a number of books, pro and con, about the often mysteriously depicted Master Fard Muhammad, by authors who secured advance documents from the FBI's "Anti-American Activities" files. While they acknowledge the government's prejudicial predisposition, they draw almost exclusively upon these records as source material and still claim to provide a clear and unbiased image of the man! I ask these well-meaning authors how could the teachings of such a morally bankrupt individual, as they portray; could have ever laid the foundation for one of the most powerfully impacting, black, social-economic religious movements in America?

Upon Master Fard Muhammad's return arrival to the country on July 4, 1930, he had been educated at the University of California-Los Angeles. He was reportedly fluent in some 16 different languages and several dialects. This was not uncommon in this time period, where multi-lingualism was necessary for travelers and traders and almost nobody lived in a monolingual world. It was not unusual for Jewish settlers from areas now known as Poland and Russia to come to Palestine speaking 16 to 18 languages. Master W. D. Fard, having been raised under the Khalifah state (as characterized by his doctrine), the seeds of which took root in our community. Like his father, Master Wallace D. Fard Muhammad first became known as a cloth merchant. Using the familiarity afforded to a door-to-door salesman, he began introducing his adversarial ministry to members of America's Black communities in this country's great (auto) industry city of Detroit. This was shortly after Garvey's Pan-African back-to-Africa approach as focused around a ship he called the African Star, a movement predicated upon Garvey's belief that Blacks would never win their full Citizenship rights of equality in this Country, many of those who embraced this view, today make-up the greater part of the Liberian Government, rich in diamonds and other natural minerals.

Grandfather's given name was Elijah Poole. He was born within the first two weeks of October 1897, in Cordel County, Georgia. The Bible in which the family's birth dates were recorded was lost when fire consumed the log cabin home. He was the son of a sharecropper and a Baptist minister, the seventh of thirteen children (Sam, Charles, William Jr., Tommie, Kallatt, Johnnie, James, John Herbert, Hattie, Lula, Anna, and Emma) born to Marie and William Poole. He taught

**Mr. and Mrs., The Hon. Elijah Muhammad &
Sister Clara Muhammad**

himself to read from the Bible. At the age of 19, he had become a forty-cent-a-day plowboy, having received only a fourth-grade level of education. In 1918, with the aid of horse-drawn wagon, Granddad and Grandma, at 21 and 18 years old, were forced to elope in order to marry. Great Grandfather Clardon (Grandmother Clara's father) was a land owner versus my Granddad being the son of a sharecropper. Like any man, he wanted his daughter Clara to marry a man who showed the promise of giving her a good life. Grandfather, young Elijah, went to his father-in-law making wide-eyed promises that he came to share with us, promises that even he could not have believed, although he was later blessed to give her all that he had promised and even more. He migrated to Detroit in 1923 with his father, Great Grandfather William, and his older brother, Sam, to seek work in the auto industry. Great Grandfather said he had to get his boys out of the South. Two weeks after a young white girl had recanted her rape charges against a young man, the townsmen had murdered him. Grandfather told us of his having witnessed this event in the town square, the brutal burning of a black man. As the man attempted to eat the dirt and ashes to escape the pain and agony, they kicked it from his hand!

Great Grandfather, Grandfather and his older brother Sam were the advance members of the family to leave Georgia seeking a better life. Once they secured employment at the Chevrolet plant, the wives came shortly after. Over the next few years, through the great stock market crash of 1929, Grandfather held several jobs after the one at General Motors Chevrolet, including working and supervising railroad men laying tracks. Grandfather's supervisory skills were quite apparent, as he quickly gravitated to such positions.

Dual Lynchings

What fueled and perpetuated such a level of Racist Hatred?

SIX

The Underlying Psychological Redemptive Factors Of Fard's Doom's Day Machine

America's "roaring twenties" closed an era for the migrant Poole family. Relatively speaking, they were having some hard times. This may have been one reason they were attracted to the Islamic doctrine that Professor or Master W. D. Fard was soon to introduce them. Master Fard's doctrine stated that he had built a spaceship as spoken of in "Ezekiel's Vision." This was perhaps only to give us pride and closure while removing us from the final battle. He would tell of having masterminded it and sent it up in 1929 from one of Japan's five islands. This ship was a half-mile in diameter. It was called the "Mothership" because it carried 1,500 smaller craft. Since it was not truly understood why the American stock market had fallen, the story about this huge craft frightening everybody was given plausible context. In years to come, some of the media would come to characterize Grandfather as an Old Testament's Doom's Day Prophet.

At that time (1930) Grandfather found employment virtually non-existent. He had a wife and five children to feed and clothe: My eldest uncle Emmanuel, 9; Aunt Ethel, 7; Aunt Lottie, 5; Uncle Nathaniel, 3; and Dad Herbert, only a year old. Dad received his

The Honorable Elijah Muhammad

name from one of the attending nurses in the hospital where he was born. Faced with such impoverished circumstances, Grandmother, quite embarrassed after childbirth, asked the nurse to give her newborn a name. And so she did, naming Dad after the country's newly elected president, Herbert Hoover. Grandmother vowed never to give any of the boys Grandfather's name until he had made something of himself. They were living in a shotgun house, meaning that the doors had been removed by the landlord when they found themselves unable to pay the rent. The children played in the streets of Detroit and they were even unable to buy them shoes for their feet. Grandmother found work cleaning in one of the wealthy white areas of the city. Reflecting on these most depressing days, Grandmother would come to confess, "There were times I thought to call all of the children to take a nap and just put my head in the oven and then turn on the gas."

One of Grandmother's lady friends brought a man around to the house who sold fabrics and a red clothe that some of them were putting in their windows. Grandmother told of how she was sitting on her back porch one afternoon when she first saw "The Savior" (a reference that she would use emphatically) Master W. D. Fard Muhammad. "He looked to me like a poor white man." His first question was, "Where is brother? (Grandfather)." Her reply: "He's in the house asleep, lying across the bed drunk as a coot." Grandfather had taken to heavy drinking of alcohol. Master Fard then extended an invitation for them to come to one of the Sunday hall meetings.

Having no one to keep the children, Grandfather and Grandmother were not able to attend the meeting together. Grandfather arrived at the Sunday meeting hall, an afternoon that would change our family forever upon his first opportunity to hear Master Fard Muhammad's address. Right after the lecture concluded, Grandfather, like many others, approached the speaker to shake his hand for acceptance. At that point Grandfather acknowledged

Fard as "The Deliverer" to our people. Under the tutelage of his Arabian born mentor, Grandfather came to receive international acclaim for his work in the Black community, using the religion as a vehicle of social-economic "self-reliance," with slogans such as "Up you mighty race, you can accomplish what you will!" Grandfather was established in the faith as "Muhammad' or the living example to his people and carried the title "The Messenger of Allah." Grandfather was first called by the name Brother or Minister Elijah Kareem. However, he later earned the right to carry the name God gave to the Revelator of the Holy Quran (May the Peace and Blessings of Allah be upon him), the same last name as Master Fard Muhammad, his teacher and mentor for some three years. At the time when Grandfather first began attending the meetings along with his brother, Uncle Kallott, Master Fard's principal minister was Brother Ghulam Ali.Grandfather very shortly requested to attend the minister's classes.

At one of Brother Minister Ghulam Ali's meetings, one of the followers approached the minister in a clandestine manner, holding a shopping bag and then saying in a low voice "I've got me one." When Minister Ghulam Ali looked over in the bag he learned that this brother was carrying the decapitated head of a blue-eyed blond-haired Caucasian! In years to come (1972) Grandfather would testify to Prophet Muhammad, Ibn Abdullah (SAAW) of 1,400 years ago , "He was a white-man!" Master Fard's literature, circulated as a small booklet at that time, referred to: "The Blue-eyed blond-haired Caucasian as Yacob's grafted devil," and went on to state "...if you bring three devil's heads, you shall receive $10,000 and a trip to the Holy City of Mecca in Arabia."

"Minister Ghulam Ali was quickly relieved of his duties as minister (as this incident resulted in the arrest and interrogation of all the members of "Muhammad's Temple") for not

Oil by Jesus Muhammad-Ali (1969)

having explained this reference to decapitation as only an allegory. Grandfather was then named to the principal ministerial role under Master Fard. After this tragic event, it was made quite clear all of the ministers must close with this statement:**"When you leave here, don't do anything to anyone that you would not have done to yourself."** Having one from among us (an American so-called Negro) as the principal minister, for Master Fard, was quite essential: A minister who could put the teachings in a language that we as a people could understand and relate to, **"knee to knee and toe to toe,"** as he would put it, emphasizing to brothers, **"You have an understanding. Put it in the best language brother."** Grandfather told of an incident when Master Fard approached this big Black man on the steps of the church, declaring, "I'm your Jesus." The man knocked Master Fard down those steps. He even lost a tooth.

These two men, Master Fard and Grandfather, just happened to be about the same height, 5'6", and even weighed the same, 145 pounds. This worked out well. When Grandfather had a sudden need for a dress suit, Master Fard was found most accommodating. Of all the restrictive laws to adjust to, no pork, one meal a day, no alcoholic beverages of any kind (we as a people are prone to excess), the biggie for Grandfather was to kick the habit of smoking. He would fan the room when he heard Master Fard was coming. Master Fard and his staff, his secretary Aunt Bernastine (Uncle Big John's wife), would also accompany them from city to city. On the road, they were often together around the clock. Professor Fard was known not to need more than two hours of rest and was also said to have been as light and easy on his feet as Fred Astaire on the dance floor. As a young man, he was known to have been a very strong swimmer.

My Aunt Lottie, who at the time was all of 8 years old, shares this account of the day when Master Fard received the "Official Notice" from U.S. Immigration. "Master Fard Muhammad arrival at the house was much like any other day. However, after a short time had passed, for the first time she came to hear her daddy crying." There had been a time when Master Fard had threatened to leave and never return to Grandfather's. He asked the Professor, who he had been told, had all of the answers to his questions. Grandfather came to ask, "How was the first Sun created?" His reply, with his eyes glaring in an awful sense of rage, was "If you ask me that question again, I will leave and never return!" So when the day came when he was faced with Master Fard's leaving, Aunt Lottie spoke of her sadness on hearing the penetrating hurt of her dad's sobbing as soon as he learned that his friend had to go away.

Of Grandfather's little girls, Aunt Lottie had come to share a very special place with her dad. When Aunt Lottie was only just months old, she had developed rickets. She quoted her mother as saying, "Lottie, you were so little and helpless, like a little bird." As Auntie explained, Grandfather found her undeniably abandoned by Grandmother. Grandfather would walk for great distances to take her to a treatment center where he would rub oil on her little limbs under a hot lamp.

The letter from the U.S. Immigration came in the spring of 1934. Master Fard was told if he did not leave within 14 days he would face deportation. "Due to unrest stemming from his activities in the Negro community." Grandfather and the family had moved twice. They were in a much nicer home, in a more respectable area of Detroit. Master Fard summoned the Minister's staff and told them to obey Grandfather as Supreme Minister and Uncle Kallott as Supreme Captain. They did not need him any more. The afternoon of May 24, 1934 would be the last time they would see Master Fard with the exception of Grandfather. A week or so later Grandfather received a telegram; Master Fard wanted him to come and see him in a Chicago jail. He told Grandfather that the family should move to Chicago. "Chicago" retained its Native American Indian name, meaning "The Mighty." The Native Americans equated wind with the Great Spirit. Master Fard then told Grandfather why he sent for him. "I wanted you to see me here behind these bars. If you follow me, this is where you will find yourself."

The person that Grandfather and others had come to know by the name Master W. D. Fard Muhammad was reported to have taught in South Africa prior to bringing his ministry to this country. However, having taught them he was "Noble Drew Ali," the Third Khalif (May Allah be Pleased with him) reincarnated, Master W. D. Fard then taught them that the black tablet placed on the prayer rug of many Muslims was in homage to Ali. He taught that Ali was that long-awaited one who would raise the "Black Stone," symbolizing the Black man. This information was actually taken from a book published in Europe which was given to me in November 1968 by a Saudi Sheikh and linguist, Mohammad Al Mana, a native of India, a highly respected companion to Imam King Abdul Azziz Al Saud and a former member of his Cabinet. Grandfather's response to these disclosures was in this way: "It does sound like something Master Fard told me when he was in some swamp wearing those big hip boots and there were all of these big snakes."

Reincarnation, or the metaphysical approach to spirituality, was bonded to the fabric of Grandfather's delivery. While quoting from the Bible or Holy Scripture: "...and the Prophets shall be reborn around him, as the sheep knew the voice of the shepherd," or calling forth the subconscious mind from the sea of souls. The subconscious mind represents nearly ninety percent of our brain's force of presence (Our Angel and Jinn, guardians). None of the Eastern cultures or those of Africa, like the languages and dialects of Swahili and Arabic are so suited to

The Capital Building

the expression of these concepts, have any problem with the concept of reincarnation. Biblically, David is reported to have been a tall fair-skinned redheaded man. Reincarnation is merely a way of explaining the noted relationship that man is invariably molded by the will of our subconscious minds, given character by our view of life while the word was given as a vehicle of the spirit. The Holy Bible refers to the subconscious as the "ghost" in the context of "He gave up the ghost." Our subconscious mind is of the ghost of Adam (May Allah Grant him with the Mercy). We are all his progeny, an extension of he to whom God Almighty entrusted "the breath of life" or mankind's level of perception. In the context of lecturing, Grandfather would say, "They never taught us the true meaning of religion" and then put it in another way, "No one wanted to awaken the sleeping Lion, because you may be his first meal," establishing a productive psychologically reinforcing dialogue with the believers, often on a subconscious level. "We love the devil, because he gives us nothing." Often we judge others by our own heart. We refuse to believe our kindnesses won't be returned in kind, subjugating us to usury.

Grandfather, a very meek-mannered man, aggressively stepped forth to champion such a philosophy in the name of religion during the 30's, as he hated to see his people's level of physical and psychologal subjugation to Whites, after serving them as chattel for 15 brutal generations. He openly taught Black people Master Fard Muhammad's philosophy that Whites were a race of "Yacob's grafted" devils, a grafting of a race out of the naturally evolved Creation, a biblical verse ("Let us make man" however, this is man speaking.) in which there were two germs (seeds). As God told the Holy Prophet Moses (May Allah be pleased with him) to put his hand in his bosom, when he pulled it out, it was speckled. He then told him to put it in a second time. It became as it was originally. The grafting was said to have been done 6,000 years ago on the island of Pelon or Patmos

The Hyde Park Mansion

in the Aegean Sea. Biblically, "...and John was in the spirit on the Lord's Day, on the Island of Patmos." Grandfather also put it this way: "Only a devil could come and make you hate your own Black flesh!"

Grandfather wanted it clear: The Creator, who hung all those stars out there, no, He didn't bring this on us. It was by our own hand! Yacob was a black man who chose to graft out of us the Caucasian race. A great many people felt that Grandfather would merely wind up being a hump in some farmer's field. As he would put it, "The job calls for a man like Moses!"–Moses, who parted the Red Sea—"The sea we must part is blood as it applies to our people and the ways of their open enemy, the Caucasian White race." Respect breeds respect: "Our seeking to marry with them only provides them with justification for their killing us when the Black man has the dominant germ." Yes! In 1972 U.S. President Richard Millhouse Nixon offered to provide massive aid to the Honorable Elijah Muhammad's Nation of Islam. The president's message to Grandfather: "I don't care what you teach them, look at what you are making out of your people!" However, the prerequisite was that Grandfather turned over all of his records.

The day of the Honorable Elijah Muhammad's passing (May Allah Grant him the Mercy), February 25, 1975, the organization known as the Nation of Islam had amassed assets estimated at $80 million and to entail: 750,000 acres of farm land in Alabama; a $1 million newspaper press located on Chicago's South 26th and Federal Street; three ships under lease off the coast of Peru (terms: $360,000, renewable per 90-days), the largest importer and marketer of whiting fish; a $1.2 million Lockheed Jet Star, four engine, ten passenger private plane; not to name each of the nearly 200 temples, grammar and high schools, the Universities of Islam Nationally. One should include appropriately, in cities across the country, groceries or supermarkets and bakeries.

Master W. D. Fard Muhammad

In 1972, I became the manager of one such bakery, Shabazz here on Chicago's South Side. We had four trucks on the street serving hundreds of grocery stores and supermarkets City wide, like Jewel Foods and a number of Certified and Cooperative markets, to include what is termed "Mom and Pop" groceries, and many were Arab markets as well. Grandfather would say, "The people know us through our services in the community, businesses of all types."

What is exemplary is how the Nation of Islam rose to a level of achievement under such adverse circumstances that became in the 70's a beacon of encouragement and a living testimony to Black self-reliance. *We need leadership by positive example. No one can undermine us the way we do one another. We appear to be in a self destruct mode.* If we, as a people are the handy work of our former White slave Masters, then he has certainly did his job because we've taken over. Just look at the level of Black on Black crime in our Communities; it is truly heart breaking! At Chicago's Cook County Jail facility complex located on the Southside at 26th and California, tax payers are warehousing nearly19,000 pre trial detainees at an average cost of some $40,000.00 a year (Full Medical benefits, clean facilities, with air condition and color televisions accommodations while providing the breading grounds for gang recruitment).

In 1959, there were 3 prisons in State of Illinois; today we have 29 with on going construction in place. The Nation of Islam addressed many of the woes and psychological and spiritual wounds of America's disenfranchised Black Community. Forming a competitive social model or microcosm for Black Christian Ministers, as today such an outreach for housing and other forms of Community development has become common place. Achievement under highly adverse circumstances is a testimony to the soundness of the philosophy behind it, which was whole-heartedly embraced by many. It addressed many woes and psychological and spiritual wounds of America's disenfranchised Black community. The philosophy and organizational structure attracted and even produced such internationally renowned Black leaders as today's highly controversial Minister Farrakhan, the outspoken three-time Heavy Weight Champion Muhammad Ali, and Malcolm X (El Hajji Malik Shabazz). One fact remains: He, Allah is the One by his Mercy, who brought them to become Muslim and receive this message, He, Whose The Grand Architect of the hearts of men (and women), The Lord of Host.

Although not all of those affected by the message left their churches, their lives or their spirits, the way that they think, was impacted by these men and their gripping testimony of conviction and faith. In the 1950s, the Nation of Islam members would address each other as "Black-man." This is common today, but if you were to address an American so-called Negro of that era in such a way then, before doing so, you should be prepared to defend yourself! It would become quite clear, even upon first impression, this was a message that had to be received as it was delivered, aggressively!

The six-foot, four-inch fair-skinned red-headed Black-man who came to be known as "Malcolm X" or Brother Minister Malcolm in the fifties and early sixties, with his piercingly embittered voice, bound by a pervasively distinctive personal sense of affront as to the condition of our people, provided such an aggressive delivery. Yes, there was cunning, but there was more. Whatever it was, for many it was by Allah's mercy. Programs like Mike Wallace's national television talk show; **"The Hate That Produced The Hate!"** Took the Nation of Islam's message from back rooms to the living rooms of America. Yes, there were other aggressive and outspoken ministers, about half a dozen or so; thus, Malcolm felt the pressure of wanting to be out front and in the forefront.

The Hyde Park Palace

The Nation's Jet

Muhanmmad's University of Islam / Elementary & High School

The Nation's Sales & Office Building

He is a Brother who was known to even take his case of debate or argument to the forefront. He is a Brother who was known to even take his case of debate or argument to the campus of Harvard University. Massive train rides were organized, with hundreds of Muslims coming from the North, traveling to the South, with banners and streamers of their mission, pitting the bleeding liberal against the unyielding red neck mentality of the South.

Unlike the Freedom Riders, Muslims were not under instruction to ever be reduced to beg from the white man. Nor were they about to let anyone spray fire hoses on them or let someone sick a dog on them either. They were not "nonviolent." They received regular martial arts training, which included how to fight dogs to the death, if it was brought to that point, be it one way or the other. This state of mind or discipline applied to law enforcement as well: "You don't need a gun, they are bringing you your gun!"

Minister Wallace D. Muhammad, at 41 years of age, stood with Brother Minister Malcolm X (May Allah Grant him the Mercy) in his bid for leadership in 1963, then on February 25, 1975, to succeed Grandfather (The Hon. Elijah Muhammad, at 77 years of age) upon his passing (May Allah Grant him the Mercy and Bless him with the Paradise). Minister W. D. Muhammad was the fifth son and seventh child born in a household of six boys and two older sisters. In his most formative years, he had very little contact with his father. This was his lot until he reached the age of 12. My Grandfather, the Hon. Elijah Muhammad, came to spend five years in a Federal Penitentiary at Millings, Michigan, alongside many of the followers who refused to submit to induction into the Armed Services during World War II. They were labeled "Anti-American" and "pro-Japs" as newspapers throughout the country reported their arrests.. Grandfather, at the age of 43 in the spring of 1941,

Uncle Imam Wallace Deen Muhammad & His Mother, Sister Clara Muhammad (October 30, 1933)

despite his family of eight children and his being well past draft age, was arrested. One of the charges was sedition, as a religious doctrine taught to citizens. This charge was not supported by law. Yet Grandfather and many others toughed it out, including 19-year-old Emanuel, his eldest son.

"Pro-Japs" was an interesting anti-American handle for the government to coin, giving Grandfather and his followers such a repulsive stigma. However, if you study the history of Hitler's swastika, an image was taken from ancient Asian Zen temples, dating back to 3,400 B.C., you will find that the Zen philosophy states that when dealing with an enemy you take the weapon that they have forged against you and then use it on them. Hitler's "ultimate solution," Death, deemed the ultimate statement of God's having forsaken a person or a people. In the context of "avenging Christ" Adolph and his Nazi Party inflamed the prevailing anti-Semitism to win support in Germany. Hitler first called attention to how their Jewish co-workers "gravitated towards intellectual vocations" and perpetuated statements of Jewish control of all of the factors which frustrated the workers.

This prejudice was exacerbated by the traditional framing of the Biblical account of Christ's crucifixion (May Allah be pleased with him). Christ was shown as condemned by the Jews or the Pharisees (law givers) as Christ had rebuked them for their self-righteous behavior, finding them guilty of applying the Mosaic Law in such a way as to prostrate the people while setting themselves up as lords over them. Then the Jews "used" the Romans to bring the Christ to death (May Allah's peace be upon him), as a tool of bringing earthly shame. Hitler then applied the zen swastika approach of using their law on them in the same way.

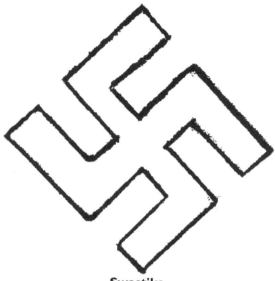

Swastika

From Science

Professor Albert Einstein, born in Germany in 1879, was : known to have been an outspoken humanitarian and a profoundly religious man, as he was offered the position of becoming the Zionist State's first Prime Minister, Professor Albert Einstein's likeness can be found on Israeli currency today. World renown as a theorist physicist whose insights can be found in his highly acclaimed theory of relativity ($E=MC^2$), first published in a scientific journal in 1906, ultimatly led to the development of atomic power. He said that he had first perceived these concepts at 16 years of age, in what he stated was "much like a dream-like state." This theory provided scientists with the fundamental insights as to the atom's make-up. However, the theory does not provide instruction as to how this energy can or should be unleashed. It was left to others to develop the constructive and the destructive aspects of atomic power.

The U.S.'s nuclear program had everything to do with its covert information network and Hitler's neurotic search for such a power, after having studied many of the old Hebrew texts, after all the bad press, the Germans produced the first atomic explosion, the jet aircraft and the world's first automobile, the Mercedes Benz. During World War II, America's approach, with the assistance of the allies, was simply to abduct these scientists. While in the first book of the Holy Prophet Moses (May Allah be Please with him), we read in Genesis the first thing formed by God Almighty was "light"; while an understanding of its nature forms the basis of Professor Albert Einstein's famous **theory of relativity** or the C squared portion of the formula represents light multiplied times itself. For me

Albert Einstein

this was a linkage to Master Fard Muhammad's instructing us to study light, while in our Quranic studies it is revealed that the Angel's were created from light, the Ginn from fire and man from the clay of the Earth. It wasn't until Christ (May Allah be pleased with him), provided insight on this subject, while they were looking for God's Power off on some mountain! In the Gospel, the lady from Samara standing by the well offers Christ some water and then questioned him about his being of those who prayed in Jerusalem. In reply he stated: "There shall come a time when man shall pray anywhere. God's Power is like that of the mustard seed, it is the smallest but from it comes the tallest of the vegetation. For God's power can be found in the smallest of things (Atom is a Greek word, meaning the smallest of things)".

In 1942, it was at Chicago's Fermi Laboratory where the first sustained nuclear reaction occurred and the resulting massive destructive atomic bomb dropped on two Japanese cities in 1945. We must remember that the Holy Prophet Moses (May Allah's Peace be upon him) was raised in the house of Egypt's pyramid builders, a technology that even today one wonders why we cannot duplicate even one of them! Sad to say it, but before the time Professor Einstein's theory was used as a tool of push button mass murder, if you were to visit a "good upstanding" white Anglo-Saxon home, it was common to find a sign on the front door: **"Negroes, Jews and dogs, back door."**

Many U.S. towns, particularly in the pan-handle regions of Texas had signs "Nigger, don't let the sun set on you here." The more "subtle" North merely had the so-called "Restrictive Covenant," which was a homeowner's agreement not to sell or rent not only to Negroes, but Jews, Catholics, and other "minorities." This was not declared illegal until 1954. The restrictive segregation of home ownership, access to capital, etc. etc. has continued in newer and more virulent forms until this day.

Ali, after receiving notice from the draft board

Muhammad Ali with Sultan Muhammad (on far right) in the Mid-East.

The Nation of Islam's first order of the day was to call attention to America's institutional racism. President Reagan said attention to America's institutional racism. President Reagan said it in this way, "before we knew we had a racial problem." There was no problem if one was born to the condition (as in ignorance is bliss). As Muhammad Ali (Clay) would say, "Why is it, angel food cake is white and devil food cake is chocolate?" The likeness of this in reverse usage is found in Grandfather's aggressively teaching our Black community what our Savior, Master Fard, had taught him: the white man was the devil. At the time Hitler was murdering millions of other white people. The White man's coming to unleash the destructive power of the atom bomb, such a power was foretold by the Gospel's closing chapter of Revelation, as Christ's vision (May Allah be Pleased with him) has the likeness of today's arsenal of nuclear submarines and Jet planes that pack their smart bombs and nuclear payloads that can rain death upon millions with a single blast! Yet today, we have all kinds of diversions, football, basketball and what is Hollywood's latest craze that we just must see! We must become focused and give account of our selves, understanding just what day we live in.

During the years 1934 to 1941, Grandmother would simply say, if asked of Grandfather's whereabouts, "Brother, is in the bush." He traveled for seven years from city to city, teaching and setting up temples. At first this sometimes meant riding under the train or in the baggage area. Those years ended with his five years of incarceration. These were the twelve formative years of Wallace D.'s bonding and character building, spent with his parental guardians, being his mother or grandmother, formally called Sister Clara Muhammad (May Allah Grant her the Mercy). Sister Clara was a very strong-willed sister about 102 lbs, standing all of five feet tall. She was an aggressive disciplinarian with a white-glove attitude about cleanliness when

Granddad, Prof. Uncle Akbar, and Father Jabir Herbert

Muhanmmad's University of Islam / Elementary & High School

My Mom and her only daughter, Safiyya.

it came to her housekeeping agenda. Then, when it came to the kitchen, she was either cooking herself weeks before the dinner and storing it in one of her huge freezers, or supervising her two cooks, sisters, in preparation for the huge monthly Ministers' Meetings and Dinners. Living in the coach house just in back of the 19-room mansion in Chicago's Kenwood-Hyde Park area at 4847 South Woodlawn, we were often at her back door, Grandmother had us on our hands and knees with a toothbrush cleaning around the baseboard of the kitchen floor. She was a real task master. She made sure that we knew how to clean. Once, Grandfather was coming to make an inspection of the bakery. The clean-up detail belonged to my brother Elijah and I, at 14 and 15 years old, respectively. Grandfather remarked, "You boys clean like women."

I was born to a 17-year-old mother, Antonia Larrieu, the oldest of six and the only girl. We came to live at Grandpa's for four years. Mom was raised a Catholic and was married the year before. Mom was named after her grandfather, Anthony Bouté, my great grandfather, a Turkish whaler who was killed at sea (May Allah Grant him with the Mercy), in 1919 when grandmother Ester was but four years old. The bond between Dad's mom, Clara, and Mother was established out of respect. Much of that respect was born out of the role Grandmother Clara played in those very early years, when her household consisted of five boys and two girls. There were white suits on Sundays and bald (shaved) heads to go around for all six of the young Muhammad boys. Grandmother was also known to take the buggy whip to the older boys if they thought to challenge her rules. It was also Sister Clara who was often called to go before the believers on Sunday, to read the letters Grandfather would write them from his prison cell.

This female-dominant family structure would come to have a profound impact on Wallace D.'s leadership. This was brought to bear in his unwillingness to accept the hurt dealt his mother when he learned of his father's having chosen to lead a polygamous life (in contradiction to his espoused doctrine for the followers).In perspective, the greatest stumbling block for Grandfather's original eight children appears to have been the acceptance of the advent of Granddad's other children aspiring to succeed to leadership, a nightmare for the prideful. Wallace's childhood exposure to Professor Jamil Deabb, an Egyptian from whom he received his Arabic classes, provided many family members with an explanation as to the basis for Wallace's abandonment of Grandfather's or "The Savior" Master Fard Muhammad's approach to the faith.

In 1959 his three sons, Herbert (my Dad), Wallace D., and his youngest Akbar (from Grandmother's eight children) accompanied their father on *Hajj* to Mecca (a requirement for every Muslim, at least once in their life time). This became a three-month long journey during which Grandfather was received in Cairo as an honored guest by Egypt's beloved President Gamel Abdul Nasser, and returned to the country via Washington D.C., to be met by what was best described as a gala-like ticker tape parade down Pennsylvania Avenue, with thousands of his followers lining the route from the airport.

Uncle Wallace D., shortly after having made Hajj, was given a ministerial post in Philadelphia. Such an appointment gave a Minister a lot of power. In the hierarchy of the Nation of Islam, Grandfather was much like an Emperor and the powers of his Ministers were like those of governing kings or regional viceroys (in the Turkish model). All the Ministers had to travel to Chicago for the monthly Ministers' meetings, at which they submitted their reports to Grandfather in person at the dinner table. One meeting, the East Coast regional, would be held on the first of the month and the other, the West Coast regional, on the fifteenth:Captains and a member of their Temple staff, generally the secretary, often came to read and submit their

Headquarters of Muhammad Speaks -Early days

Front of building in recent days

report. "FOI" is the acronym that stands for the name given by Master Fard to the brothers, referring to them as the "Fruit of Islam." The sisterhood counterparts were "Muslim Girls Training" (MGT) and "General Civilization Class" (GCC).

The women dressed in long white satin robes, fully covered, with only the face and hands exposed or *Kejab* as in the Arabic reference. What an American Blackman will not do if he canfind a way to control his woman! One must address this crippling cultural flaw, whose roots are found in a generational spiral, passed down from the days of America's chattel slavery. The advent of the Black man finding his woman's respect for the brotherhood was one of the most powerful keys of the Nation of Islam's success! "The respect given your woman, the mother of your children and their first teacher, and so the cornerstone of the family unit, culturally translates to become the respect extended us as a people!" The word "control" must not be taken out of context: control by mutual adherence to righteous conduct. This of course meant that the man, too, must adhere to the code and clean himself up, while giving respect is not always given. It must be earned. This meant discipline: The FOI classes on Saturday mornings meant drilling, exercises, push-ups and a full martial arts regimen—mind, body and soul approach. This included newspaper detail.

Muhammad Speaks reached sales of nearly a million copies per week, its revenue became the backbone of nearly all the economic programs via Granddad's central management approach. Each FOI was required to buy at least 300 newspapers per edition, at a slightly reduced price to encourage sales. When Wallace D. assumed office in 1975, he had armed security at all times, even at family meetings. Security who'd look you deep in the eyes, with an anticipated glee of introducing you to your mortality. He would very shortly institute sweeping changes, including lambasting Grandfather with statements

**A million dollar printing press just south
of Chicago's Downtown.**

like "My father did not believe in God." A statement he made at a dinner speech at the Abu Dhabi Hilton (an Arabian Gulf State), in December of '76, while the honored guest of Sheikh Dr. Sultan Mohammad bin Al Quassimi with three Ambassadors in attendance. The Chief (as he was called in those days) while refering to our Community (or Oulema) as "The Body Christ". In Uncle W.D.'s first year in office the FOI and the MGT was promptly dismissed (for many the belonging came to represent a way of life)! This also marked the economic downfall of Grandfather's lifetime effort and that of many believers who heeded his call (May Allah Bless each and every one).

The Nation of Islam's FOI and MGT were taught to aggressively address and reinforce strong family values in our Community. "We shall always be governed by others until we learn to be fair and just in our dealing with one another." Today for many a Black man, it's his wife's razor-sharp emasculating tongue before his children. The seeds of this total lack of respect were surely planted by the White man's "peculiar institution" of slavery in this country: "Destroy the family unit!" This was absolutely necessary for the unique chattel slavery practiced only in the U.S. of A. This is something many American Blacks yet struggle with daily: Justice in our dealing with one another! The five-pointed star was placed in our flag to symbolize Justice. In English, "Jesus" means Justice. "Up from slavery, my Brother!" As a people we are faced with many many types of stressors in big city life and so many injustices within, without and among us.

The law enforcement system, from the foot patrolman on up to the Supreme Court Justices, intrusively overshadows our Community. If a Black is murdered by a Black it is not aggressively addressed, rather indexed as a common occurrence, mundane. According to a report provided by a Chicago City coroner, on any given night there can be found six out of eight young

Muslim Girls Training (MGT)

The FOI, the Fruit Of Islam

Black men's bodies down there, between the ages of 14 to 25, giving rise to the national statistic (as an insurance company rep will tell you): A Black male child in America is given but a 50% chance of ever reaching his 25th birthday. **This is horrible and can hardly be deemed acceptable for a people, for whom a Georgia State survey shows we have an annual buying power of nearly a half Trillion dollars.** Is it only materialism for us? Chicago proper with a population of 3 million and another 5 million, if we include its suburbs, a City with the boast of being second in the nation served by only one trauma Center at Cook County, as any fireman cinfronted with the frustration of rushing someone he has risked his life saving when moments are precious. On any weekend, just pickup a camcorder, you'll find that Chicago's Cook Count Hospital looks like a hospital in a war zone. In the sixties we were burning down our communities, demanding our "fair share" of the American apple pie. **Now, what are those of us, who have been given our fair share plus, doing with it, as far as our collective selves?**

Just as we want Whites in this country to understand our point of view, we must also try and meet them at least half way. Today's American White man has inherited much to try and live down, while he also has an image to live up to. Look at this bombing in Oklahoma. Whites also are beginning to feel that this government no longer represents them. What about all of these tanks and other military equipment that came up missing? *"It's a private collection. If they try and get these arms back the country may go into another civil war!"* All on line, with PCs nationally. Just think about it for a minute. The increase in population by birth rate Blacks or non-whites in this country is 4 to 1, while the Caucasian increase is zero (-0-); they are just replacing themselves; for every one that is born one dies. Between the interracial marriages, abortions, birth control pills, and the likes, the White population is further reduced.

White backlash to Civil Rights gains

Timothy Mcveigh

The Alfred P. Murrah Building after the blast

Christ states, "As you treat the least of mine, so do you treat me." Yet , we have countless millions of babies thrown in the trash can, while they are still moving, in abortion clinics across the country. In a country that is supposed to be a democracy, with one man one vote, why should the governing Caucasian people seriously concern themselves with us murdering each other in our gangland communities?

Then, we have our economically liberated or successful Blacks who appear to be preoccupied with assimilating into a dominant White culture, adopting their values, attitudes, or spirit, even about their own people rather than reaching back to their old communities and trying to establish a way out for their trapped brothers and sisters. Lucifer or Ibles spoke to God, "I could get into him (Adam or man)", This left man unwittingly prey to doing Satan's work! Remember, the Book says that the accursed one took down with him a third of the Angels. Do we mirror our own hearts desires or do we merely seek the acceptance of the dominant or popular will of those around us, a culture whose moral values are constantly being degraded, "Of the people and by the people ?" *We find many of the immigrant Arab merchants selling swine, liquor and even some of the most explicit forms of pornography intrusively placed at the checkout counter.* As they flee the oppressive tyrants of their homelands, seeking liberty and safe haven under the banner of Christian America's red, white and blue, knowing that the Jewish State is anchored in this country's support, they give service to a passionate cry against the Zionist. As a part of an Arab credo: *If you are stupid, then someone is going to use you anyway, why not me?* Brotherhood is a two way street or otherwise it's usury. I don't see the Arab immigrant community knee deep in our ethnic woes!

Minister Farrakhan

Million Man March, an inter faith statement

Jesus with first born daughter, Ruth.

SEVEN

The Dining Room Table

Grandfather's dining room table was the hub of the spoke wheel that made the Nation of Islam the driving force witnessed in the Black community around the country. The "DINING ROOM TABLE" had an infamous mystique that emanated fear through most, including the family! As a child how many times had I, in a state of wonder, witnessed my dad coming out from the dining room table with his eyes all puffy and red, heading for the bathroom.

Some referred to the dining room table as where "court" was held! You could be invited to dinner and suddenly find that it was you who was becoming the dinner. (One would feel like saying, "Excuse me, please, I'll be right back in the next life.") First, Grandfather would make what would sound like a casual comment. Then one of his aides, generally one of a half-dozen Sisters from his secretarial staff dining with him each evening, would somehow extract an adverse meaning from his comment, speaking in abstract general references so you cannot quickly identify yourself as target. Breaking the rotation of the comments from the staff, embellishing the accusation, you state your

The Author and Artist, Jesus Muhammad-Ali

argument of defense in kind and in context, before it gets back around the table to Grandfather. If you do not break the rotation of comments, you have missed your chance for defense. Grandfather would then make about a half dozen projections that would logically deduce a plausible reasoning for doing what you were being accused of, to include those things that may have led you to believing you were going to get away with this dastardly deed!

I too came to serve as a member of Grandfather's "Court" in 1974, taking the empty seat at the opposite end of what had become a 24-seat main table (designed from the Biblical reference of the Elders). All of 25 years old, I was a portrait artist by trade and a student of nuclear (at the core of) physics as a part of a theological equation. Having distinguished myself in 1968, I became the first member of the Nation of Islam to become the honored guest of a reigning monarch over the Muslim's Holy Lands of Arabia, His Royal Majesty, King Fiasal bin Al Saud (May Allah Grant him the Mercy)

First, I made a portrait of His Majesty and sent it to his palace in Al Riyadah. After a few months and no reply, I sent him a letter requesting that the portrait be returned, because without even as much as a thank you note, to us that is a slap in the face! Within a week or so, from the Washington, D.C. Embassy, I received a check for five thousand dollars and a monogrammed gold wristwatch. Shortly thereafter, on a visit to Cairo in 1968, I witnessed the ravished conditions that had befallen the Egyptian people after the '67 war. Aware of the great wealth of the Saudis; knowing they were the financial backers of Egypt's failing military effort, without a visa I bought a ticket to the International oil port City of Dhahran Saudi Arabia, upon my arrival when confronted about my being without a visa! I requested to see the king as I presented them with a letter. I was carrying the letter from the king, in which it was asked that I please accept the gold watch that I

The Hyde Park Mansion & Coach Home

happened to be wearing, when the standing rule of turning a non visa passenger around was being deliberated. Shortly thereafter, Sheik Mohammed Al Mana, was summoned to question me.

I became the Sheik's personal guest for three days. During this time I came to meet with a gentleman, first introduced to me merely as the Sheik's friend. I was introduced and soon learned that this man was a former professor at the University of Chicago, just down the street from where I was raised. We became locked into a debate before the Sheik. After about 20 minutes, he concluded by saying that "I just can not believe that Islam can be successful in a country so Christianly dominated as America!" In reply, I exclaimed: "First there was one man, Master Fard Muhammad, from this land and this people," waving my hand past the Sheik, "then he came to America and taught my Grandfather and from these two men, my Grandfather (by Allah's Leave) has tens of thousands of faithful followers and millions of sympathizers in a relatively short time!

"It was 140 years after Christ (May Allah be pleased with him) was gone before they were even sure as to who he was!" After Sheik Mohammed Al Mana and I walked out of this man's office, insisting that I change my given name (after my Dad) he looked up at me as if I had my cloud parked outside and said: "I just can't believe the way he was bowing and shaking your hand!"

In closing, the professor and overseer of America's interest there at Aramco said, "If your grandfather is producing young men like yourself, I would just like to shake your hand!" It was after that meeting that my visa and the king's personal invitation was extended. Upon receipt of my telegram, Mom told me of how Granddad came from his first floor dining-room up to her third floor office where she had worked for years as his secretary treasurer to share the news with her, "He is just a baby (at 19, in November of 1968) and he can't even speak

Mother Marie / Mother of the Honorable Elijah Muhammad

their language and he took my message all the way up to the king!"

I was the second-born son. My oldest brother was named for Grandfather and my given name was for my dad. I was brought home from the hospital to Grandfather's house, where my parents lived, when I was ten days old. I lived there until I reached the age of four. In 1953 we all moved from 61st and Michigan to the 19-room Mansion on Woodlawn in the Hyde Park-Kenwood area, where our family lived in the coach house. From infancy, my closest bond was with my great grandma (the Hon. Elijah Muhammad's Mom), Mother Marie (May Allah Grant her the Mercy). She told us she saw something in my eyes. Great Grandfather, her husband William, a Baptist minister for many years, was known as somewhat of a ladies' man who would never fail to tip his hat. Great Grandfather passed in the summer of 1947. He was at the Sunday Meeting, took ill, and was taken to Chicago's Provident Hospital.

Mother Marie stood slightly stoop-shouldered. She was about 4' 10", with predominately Native American Indian features and a long white braid. It was said that she could look into your eyes and make you feel as if you were made of glass. She said, "I had what was like a dream, while pregnant with your grandfather, looking over to the window in my bedroom and seeing what looked like a light. Then I heard what sounded like a voice telling me that my unborn son was going to be the Messenger of God! I was frightened and the very next day went over by the barn and told my father Rufus. He simply told me I should give him the name "Elijah." I would sit on her little red throw pillow beside the rocking chair in her room, while she would crochet, just down the hall from Grandpa's and Grandmother's room. When she passed away (May Allah grant her the Mercy), I was eight years old. She left me with these word of wisdom (she would mostly speak from Ecclesiastics): "Son, if you don't remember anything else I've told you, remember, whatever you do, you can't go back and change it." She lived at Grandfather's until her passing, at 89 years of age, August of 1957. Late one summer evening, just about sunset, I saw Grandfather pacing the sidewalk around the Mansion, his head slightly bowed and hands clasped behind his back, certainly reflective of his pondering the weight of our mortal circumstance. Immediately recognizing that this was not a common disposition for Grandfather, I asked him was there anything wrong. He replied, "Your grandmother passed." May Allah Grant her the Mercy.

Living at the house, I saw Grandfather more often than Dad, as Grandfather worked at home. We also came to see many of the believers. One summer's evening, brother Minister Malcolm came to visit with us in the back yard. He was so tall his head touched Mom's clothesline. As it was the minister's manner, he was apologetic for his towering over us.

After Grandfather had given Uncle Wallace an appointment as Minister to Philadelphia, the powerful bonds of respect with our East Coast Regional Minister, Brother Malcolm X, became established.* On that fatal afternoon at the Audubon Ballroom, on February 21, 1965, the coroner report read: "Nineteen bullets and a shotgun blast; one of the bullets was said to have struck him in the forehead and traveled down the spine"! Then, from an eye witness: "It appeared as if everyone on the front row stood up and pulled out 38s and began firing on Malcolm, about the time of the shotgun blast"! By the time Security had taken notice of the raincoat wearing shotgun wielder coming down the center aisle it was evidential that it was too late to stop the gunman. Security had given their attention to a commotion or apparent diversion in the back of the hall. What happened to the twenty-four Police Officers of "New York's Finest" assigned to Malcolm's security remains a topic of discussion for many.**

---

*This is discussed in detail in *The Malcolm X Biography* (Full cite needed).

**Based on research secured by a former Carter White House aide.

Muhammad Ali, The Hon. Elijah Muhammad, and interviewer David Frost

Eight

Step to the Line of Media Fire:

Stepping To The Line Of Media Fire Was The Cornerstone Hype Of A Man Who America Came To Know As The Black Muslim Spokesman Minister Malcolm X Or Hajji Malik Shabazz: "The Chickens Have Come Home To Roost!"

Indicative of the statement that Minister Malcolm X made after the assassination of John F. Kennedy (November 22, 1963).

Malcolm X (Hajji Malik Shabazz), after touring the Muslim lands of the Middle East, felt that he could take the leadership; but after observing the way that the Honorable Elijah Muhammad's "Muhammad Ali" name change was met, he painfully began to realize that he had become a victim of a Credo designed as a snare for the over-zealous who rush to judgement (as it applied to Grandfather's proclaimed Messengership, simply Muhammad to his people or the living example). As for the media, this was the hype, the cornerstone of the man whom America had come to know as Brother Minister Malcolm X or Hajji Malik Shabazz: "The Chickens Have Come Home to Roost," the statement that Malcolm X, made after the assassination of President John F. Kennedy (November 22, 1963).

Malcolm X was the Regional East Coast Minister for the Honorable Elijah Muhammad's Nation of Islam in the late 50's and

Castro: Cuba's strong man digging in for a bite to eat.

President Kennedy in his famed and fatal motorcade

the late 60's. Minister Malcolm met with Cuba's strongman, Fidel Castro, in New York City's Harlem just before their revolution in 1959, when the U.S. Government was secretly providing Cuba with support. At this time of fragile diplomacy, Castro, while a guest of the United Nations in New York, went to the historic Hotel Theresa, residence for visiting musicians, entertainers, and celebrities. Described as a roach-infested hotel in media reports to confer with the Nation of Islam's National Spokesperson, Minister Malcolm X. This organization overtly espoused anti-American doctrine, proclaiming the West's interest as being morally exploitive, projecting the Latin South American countries as nothing more than playgrounds for her immoral diversions, not unlike their disposition toward Blacks, void of moral respect and regard.

Apparently no one is certain, however, what appeared to have been one of the driving factors that took Minister Malcolm over the proverbial edge can be found in Granddad's giving such a far reaching "Holy Name," like Muhammad Ali to the newly crowned Heavy Weight Champion, formerly known as "The Louisville Lip!" when Minister Malcolm first meet him as a brash young upstart. However, this name was given in a Roman Circus context, Malcolm could not fathom how the whole Muslim world embraced Elijah Muhammad's proclaimed appointment: "As it is in Heaven so shall it be on Earth!", recognizing the fan-fare the Western World places on this coveted title: "Muhammad Ali, World Heavy Weight Champion!"

After his break with my grandfather, Malcolm X established a Black Nationalist para-militant spin-off of the Nation of Islam, whose rapid growth had everything to do with Malcolm's 12 years of grooming in the Ministry led to his keen insights as to the psychology and unifying makeup of the Hon. Elijah Muhammad's Nation of Islam. These insights enabled Malcolm to have the ability to project the moral footing that would permit him to garner

support from the Nation of Islam's ranks. Nation of Islam's ranks. In order for this to take place a viable communications overlap had to be maintained, a mutual exchange that could very well have created a fatal security breach, as reflected in the revelations born out of his brutal assassination!

The coroner's report inexplicably states: 19 bullet entry wounds and a shotgun blast! Having known the Minister, personally and by reputation, and drawing from first-hand accounts of the events that afternoon, I would say that if internal security had been given direct orders or instructions from the Minister, they would have been of the strictest nature, such as: "If I become fatally hit, your job would then be to fire upon me decisively!" The problem with such an instruction, is when those who mean you harm learn of them. A would-be gunman with such knowledge would be assured of those few seconds needed to make a get away. He need look only for the time and the opportunity to deliver that fatal shot. And, gone. With prior knowledge of such an instruction, assassinating Malcolm would no longer be perceived as suicide for the would be gunman. Such prior knowledge would possibly be born out of an inner security breach.

An eyewitness stated: "It appeared as if the whole front row (known to be a designated security area) stood up and pulled out 38s and began firing on the Minister. I don't know why."

Minister Malcolm with daughters Qubilah and Attalah.

Philosophy Applied

This is also in context with the doctrine Malcolm had been taught by my grandfather, as to the account of the Christ Jesus (May Allah's Peace be on him), who decided to give up his life one rainy morning. In our daily prayers, "My life and my death are all for Allah." Allah, the name that refers to ninety-nine of Jehovah God's attributes, just as Elijah means "Jehovah is God" (Exodus 3:14). When the Holy Prophet Moses was asked he question "What is His (the Almighty's) name?" he replied, "I Am that I Am," Allah the Most Beneficent, the Most Merciful, etc. this was God's reference to the Am that I am. We were taught that Christ Jesus' surrender of his mortality (Even in crucifixion depictions there is a huge stab wound just under the right side of the rib cage, as the Holy Quran asserts, not on the cross) as a death blow to those who plotted against his life and "The Holy Gospel," staining the Jew's hands with his indelible blood (May Allah be Pleased with him).

Events joined to frame Black America's tolerance for this brutal slaying. As brother Malcolm's name became a household word in the Nation's Black community, news and social events about him could always be found in the Johnson publications *Ebony* and *Jet*. Only about two weeks before brother Malcolm's brutal murder, *Jet* featured an article with, what can only be deemed an alarming pose of a young Black girl in military training, dressed in a black leather pants-suit, squatting low while wheeling a carbine rifle into assault position. From this article and the series of photos accompanying it, we preserve Minister Malcolm's likeness depicted in his renowned pose: standing at the curtained window, shoulder-holstered weapon in place while holding a rifle, captioned, "By any means necessary" (**see page 80**).

Minister Malcolm at work in Harlem.

Muslim Girls Training (MGT) in prayer

The Hyde Park Palace

Uncle Wallace D. had gone so far as to publicly denounce Grandfather, in support of Minister Malcolm's bid for leadership. After the assassination tragedy, Wallace D. quickly returned to ask Granddad's forgiveness. Subsequently, Grandfather had to inform him that he was not able to grant such. However, Wallace was then permitted to take his request for pardon before the believers gathered for the Annual Savior's Day Convention of 1965. Even as late in Grandfather's life as December of 1974, it was just after we had left the dinner table and Uncle Elijah, Jr. had brought in a tape recording of a speech that he had ordered to be made of all of his brother Wallace's lectures. Elijah, Jr., as Assistant Supreme Captain, brought the tape along with Dr. Abdul Salaam, who was at the time over the student Ministers' classes. After the tape had finished playing, Dr. Abdul Salaam stated: "Dear Apostle (directed at Grandfather), this is not your teachings!" Afterwards, an emotionally charged debate ensued between Uncle Wallace and Dr. Salaam, with Wallace accusing Dr. Salaam of not wanting to see him and his father together.

Uncle Elijah, Jr. soon took notice of Grandfather with his hand raised to his mouth and elbow on the dinner table, poised not to comment on the tape. As Junior had brought the tape, he then informed those in dispute that they were disrespecting his father and that they all should leave as they came with As-Salaam Alaikum. I, of course, remained at my post, having never taken a seat during this hearing.

Afterwards I went to Grandfather and asked if he was ready to go up to his bedroom. He pushed back his chair and I helped him to his feet. He told me, "Let's have a seat in the brothers' front sitting-room." After being seated opposite one another, about eight feet or so apart, I said, "Wallace orders steak but he can only eat applesauce." Grandfather's reply was, "Yes son, he lost a lot ever since he turned hypocrite!" From this account of Grandfather's mind-set (December 1974), the ghost of Minister Malcolm plagued the relationship between Wallace and his father to the very day of his passing.

On the evening of January 30, 1975, during a winter vacation in Mexico, we had to rush Grandfather on the private jet to Chicago's Mercy Hospital for complications of a virus. Grandfather's lungs had been weakened in the early 60s, when he left the air conditioner on while lying across his bed on a Chicago summer evening and the temperature suddenly dropped. This left Grandfather with a chronic bronchitis that he never outlived. After he was rushed to Mercy Hospital from Mexico, I was there almost all of the time. I can say that most of the family had a chance to visit. He was originally placed on the fifth floor, but somehow he reinfected his lungs and had to be placed in the Intensive Care Unit (ICU). Nine specialists tried to deal with the problem, but they were unable to slow his heart, traumatized by spilled fluid into his lungs. He was in the ICU for about two weeks and then fell into a coma from which he never awakened (May Allah Grant him with the Mercy). My being stationed at his bedside in ICU for 20 plus hours a day, when Granddad showed no sign of presence for two weeks when approaching his personal doctor and the overseer of his care for some 20 years, Dr. Charles Williams Sr., we were informed after a prolonged exposure to the life support machine, the brain can be reduced to water. With this notice, after another two weeks on February 25th 1975, the family ordered the life support machine turned off, *listing the cause of death; complications due to congested heart failure (May Allah have Mercy upon him and Grant him the Paradise).*

Mercy Hospital, Chicago

Uncle Wallace D.'s acceptence address (Feb. 25, 1975)

NINE

NOI's Change of the Guard

The following is based on my one-on-one conversations with Uncle Wallace D. and Grandfather and frames my sense of hurt and the profound question brought to the subject of Wallace D's succession to leadership. In early December of 1974, Wallace D. attended Grandfather's last semi-National Minister's Meeting. At dinner, in the middle of the meal, Wallace D. chose to leave. I asked him about wearing clothing that was so tattered and worn. "The Ministers well provide for Grandpa, you give them the impression you're not in your father's good favor!" Uncle Wallace's reply" "Daddy doesn't give me anything for my ministering. He only gives Shirley [his wife] a small package for household expenses each month." I asked him, "Do you want me to speak to Grandpa for you?" His reply was "Yes, I would appreciate it."

The assertive nature of the article that appeared in New York City's *Amsterdam* newspaper of March 1975 was based upon a bond shared between my Granddad and me. What was amazing is uncle Wallace D. only gained knowledge of how critically ill his father's health had become after his brothers respected him enough to invite him to what was deemed an emergency meeting to discuss the advent of his dad's passing. The agenda: the future leadership of the Nation of Islam." A meeting was held at the newspaper plant warehouse on Chicago's 26th and Federal Street. At the meeting, after submitting a proposal, Dad challenged Wallace's ability to single-handedly administer the massive empire, with no credible business background, to speak of whatever. Imam W. D. would make reference to "the un-lettered Prophet." "Ume"; he would speak of this in the context of an explanation of his having alack of background in areas but otherwise given guidance by God (inferred).

When Uncle Nathaniel joined me at the hospital, he informed me of the warehouse meeting that day. He explained how, when they had asked Wallace to join with him and Dad in the leadership, Wallace, in outrage, just stormed out of the meeting (as learned) to walk a few blocks over to the *Chicago Defender* newspaper office to publicly proclaim his succession. Wallace D. stated he "had been named and groomed to be the leader!"

For me, this change of guard consisted of abandonment from Grandfather's life-long work. Along with my younger brother Sultan (May Allah Grant him the Mercy), as confidante and personal aide (often spending some sixteen or more hours each day), sharing these last five and a half months at Grandfather's side meant having first hand knowledge that Grandfather had named Dad to manage his affairs, in these words: "If I become unconscious or unable to administrate them myself, you (Herbert) are to do so." My dad later stated that he had never wanted a public life. However, when Uncle Wallace D.'s article was brought to my attention, I pressed (my) dad on the subject,

Imam W. D. Muhammad hailed as new leader.

phoning him from the hospital. "You all talk like Daddy is dead" my father said, "He may get up from there and take care of all of this himself!" Then he hung up the telephone. With this sequence of events, the family then embraced Wallace D.'s bid for leadership after the *Chicago Daily Defender*'s proclamation. There was no desire to publicly break ranks. In the name of "family unity" it was stated, so as not to default and leave the way for Farrakhan; it was uttered as the prevailing wisdom.

It was understood that the role that Wallace D. played during the Organisation's dark days of Malcolm's brutal assassination made the family's nomination for his assuming the leadership frought with uncertainty. There were many Ministers who had quite bitter memories of the dark days, of when they had truly lost one of their own. In those days, it was no secret, Wallace D. had tested the limits of their tolerance as to his own mortality. The wretched irony was that both Ministers, Malcolm and Wallace D., were aware of those followers who may be called "the hard-liners," who would stop at nothing to avenge their reproach upon the Messenger's name.

In 1975, as fate would have it, Minister Wallace D. would come to succeed his father. One of the first things he did was place his mother's name on all of the Nation of Islam Schools as a National Tribute to her. Imam Wallace D. brought us to the Sunna (Sunna, the way of the Prophet S. A. A. W.).

Wallace D. came to receive his name, months before his birth, from Master Wallace D. Fard Muhammad, who left instructions before disappearing in 1934, "If the child is a male, give him this name." Master Fard asked Sister Clara to give the child special care as (the unborn child) "shall be a helper to his father" (a statement my grandfather could personally never affirm). When Granddad, at his dining room table, was questioned on more than one occasion concerning this statement, he never challenged it but rather stated, in a very mild mannered voice: "I never heard him say this, others may have heard him say it." Out of this statement, Wallace D.'s brothers and sisters came to give him a reverent respect. However, by the same token, Minister Malcolm did also. It truly broke my grandfather's heart that Wallace used this statement of promise in an adversarial way . As a family member receiving respect from his followers, if it was brought to his attention that there was even the appearance of your abuse of one of his followers, after his reprimand, you would be left feeling, maybe, if I had never been born, I would not have offended him so!

The bond between Malcolm and my grandfather was noted in the words of those who witnessed the 6' 4" man often going to a telephone booth located in the back of the restaurant just downstairs from New York's Harlem Temple #7, that Wallace D. came to name in his honor. Minister Malcolm would often be found with tears wrapped around his chin after weeping over one of his many extended phone calls to that little man in Chicago (my grandfather).

New York, with the United Nations building and its world diplomats and heads of state, provided an international forum for the Nation of Islam's East Coast Regional Minister, Malcolm. In the late 50s it was Minister Malcolm with whom Fidel Castro came to confer. Malcolm X, a man who found White America's regard for other races as born in subjugation to them, quite repulsive and told the Cuban leader of his sense of outraged passion on the subject in many ways. In 1962, due to my Grandfather having fallen chronically ill, it was Minister Malcolm X who delivered the National Keynote Speaker at Chicago's Annual Savior's Day Convention. The collective impact felt when Minister Malcolm spoke of the hurt and suffering of our people, it was a very personal address, having a shared depth of emotion that was known to be quite moving. Undoubtedly, playing to Castro's edification, "the

Minister Malcolm and Dr. King

chickens have come home to roost" statement cost him his voice as National spokesman.

"The Royal Family," was a coined reference to my Grandfather's family given by our Brother Minister Malcolm. Yet, Minister Malcolm was seen by many of the family members as a threat, insofar as the leadership was concerned and determining who was to succeed (Dad or "The Messenger"), if the truth be told. Yes, there was a clannish paranoia on this subject. (An aristocracy, yes, but that is not Islam!) It could never truly be said that it was astounding to hear that Minister Malcolm had chosen to challenge my Granddad for the leadership. What was astounding was to hear that Minister Malcolm had chosen to slander my Grandfather, who had been his mentor, and witnessed his promise as a diamond in the rough, grooming him from the jail-house to national acclaim. As my Grandfather would say, "I did the best that I could with what I had to work with. I will give you knowledge, and Allah must Bless you with an understanding."

Uncle, Imam Wallace Deen Muhammad in full Arabian Garb.

TEN

The Philosophy of the NOI

Grandfather, just as Master Fard Muhammad, had the titles "Messenger of Allah" and "Allah in Person." These titles created a lot of unrest and confusion. However, we must first be able to accept that Master Fard, not saying why, said to Grandfather: "Put it like this (with eyes glaring), and don't you deviate! I will roll this Creation up like it's a window shade!" He no doubt intended to pit the Arab Orthodox against Grandfather's approach to the faith. During the time he spent here with Grandfather, neither of these titles had been introduced. In fact, Master Fard personally named Uncle Kallot his Supreme Captain and Grandfather Supreme Minister. When Uncle Kallot learned of the use of these titles, he went before the FOI and demanded that they denounce Grandfather as a hypocrite. Uncle Kallot's call managed to split the followers, resulting in Granddad finding it necessary to "run for his life for 7 years. One of Uncle Kallot's supporters went so far as to proclaim that "he would eat only one grain of rice a day until he took Granddad's life!" As you may recall, Grandmother Clara would only say in those days, "Brother is in the bush!"

For me, what became the contextual or inferred reference given to Master Fard Muhammad by Granddad: This was the man through whom Granddad had come to know Allah, God Almighty. To therefore proclaim an assertion and acknowledgment to the world that before meeting Master Fard Muhammad he did not know Who God Almighty was, and then proclaim himself Muhammad to his people, he made it clear that he was not the Revelator (May the Peace and Blessings of Allah be upon him). He had a duty-bound obligation to make Him, God Almighty, known to his people. Distraught on the subject, Granddad knew full well that his people were made ignorant to the knowledge of Allah, God Almighty and self, "blind, deaf and dumb!" In context: "Allah, God Almighty has always sent men to execute His Justice!"

Under the Ottomon Khalifa Rule of Mecca, Master Fard Muhammad became privy to an ancient approach to science. It was told of his being the wisest of 24 Elders, chosen by Providence, not by consensus, but rather by virtue of the manifested evidence witnessed in this awesome half mile by a half mile in diameter huge craft he dispatched, "The Mothership!" followed by the Dooms Day message of atonement to be proclaimed by Granddad in the holy Prophets' names, both the Holy Biblical and Quranic, Elijah Muhammad.

This was a philosophical approach the physics likeness of a mind laser, where two mirrors or mirrored concepts are placed parallel to one another amplifying the light between, called a population inversion process that forms a powerful beam: Represented in the two titles "Messenger of Allah" and "Allah in Person" are mirrored East / West concepts. Mexico's Montezuma (1466-1520), an Aztec Emperor who governed prior to Cortez' conquest, told his people that the likeness of the high priest was like that of a mirror, you can destroy the mirror but you cannot deny that the power of the light or knowledge that he commands is of God, or by His Leave. Not unlike Christ Jesus' title: "Rullah" or "The Spirit of Allah"is laid opposite to Prophet Muhammad's title: Rasool Allah or "Messenger of Allah."

Upon reaching college, I chose to study philosophy and had courses in Socrates' deductive reasoning. Socrates (Greece 470-399 BCE) was a philosopher who had one of the most profound influences upon the evolution of Western thought, with the advancement of his highly detailed social grid of a liberated democratic society and methodology. Like other scholars of his era, he was viewed as morally perverted and leading youth astray. For all of his trouble, at the age of 70, the governors of his day invited him to a cup of hemlock (a brew extracted from a highly poisonous flower). I knew of Socrates, having studied at Cairo, Egypt's Alezhar University, a university that boasts of being the oldest university in the world. It has the repute of being the school Jesus Christ (May Allah be plaesed with him) attended.

According to Biblical account, the Angel that appeared to Joseph told him to send Mary, Christ's mother to Egypt in anticipation of his birth. Jesus Christ's proclaimed "Holy Robe" was a robe that he (May Allah's Peace be upon him) had earned from Alazhar. He was said to have been wearing this robe, while riding a white donkey, after returning from having spent (what was termed) forty days and nights in the wilderness, in fact, Christ had walked some 1,500 miles, from Jerusalem to Egypt where he had attended school (coining the phrase "When Jesus walked", often a time of reflection). This day of Christ's return to the Holy City, has been proclaimed by the Christian world as Palm Sunday. For it was on this day, when Christ returned to the Holy city of Jerusalem, when the crowds lined the roadside placing palm branches before him and his burro. The respect that the Romans gave to the Jewish lawgivers or Pharisees had only to do with their subjugation of the masses. A leader to whom the masses bowed was not something they would risk. It was after this display, with the palms and its meaning, that the Pharisees finally took Jesus Christ's challenge of authority seriously.

This manuscript is submitted to give acknowledgment to the forceful impact that the philosophy my grandfather developed from the teachings of Master Fard Muhammad has had on the lives of so many individuals, renowned and otherwise, in this country, standing as a living testimony. However, in less than a year under Uncle Wallace D.'s leadership, Master Fard Muhammad's literature had been branded "comic book material; it's for babies!" He told the followers that they had been made fools of and so sapped their productive drive for all of the programs. "We should assimilate into the American fabric and workplaces, and join the U.S. Army!" As Imam in 1991, Wallace D. aggressively supported the cry for America's massive bombing campaign of the Iraqi people during "Desert Storm." Since, 1991, with sanctions, nearly five million Iraqis have lost their lives (May Allah Grant them the Mercy). It is becoming apparent that more Americans than admitted were also harmed in that ignominious enterprise.

Saddam, a former CIA operative, was greatly aided in this campaign by the U. S. and Germany's installation of his under-ground reinforced steel bunkers. These bunkers, that permit Saddam to sacrifice his people like lambs for slaughter, were installed during his eight year long campaign against the Iran's Imam Ayatollah Khomeini (May Allah Grant him and all of the 2 million the Mercy). Reflecting upon the beautiful manners of our Kuwaiti brothers and sisters of 1968, Saddam is a disgrace to all Islamic values and precepts, along with his barbarian 40,000 man Republican guard.

Languages

With respect to the Holy Quran, Grandfather would teach from the Bible, as he put it: "Our people have been put to sleep in that Book and we have to go in there and get them out." He taught that **"Religion is a way of life."** When he went before the body of believers he was always seen carrying both of these books. However, he told the believers that there was no falsehood in the Holy Quran; but it is too strong a medicine for them, due to the inadequacies of the English language. He further explained that English is a bastard language, having four different root languages, which places a tremendous burden on the translator who looks for a scalpel and all he can find are axes. It is a strange language in which a word may be defined by how it is framed by the sentence structure, in context, unique in many ways, with a single word often reflective of massive concepts. The spoken word of the English language has specific problems. If you were to say "I" it could be understood that you were speaking about your "eye." In the Arabic language, the name "Allah" characterizes ninety-nine of Jehovah's attributes. Jehovah is deemed the sacred and unspoken name of God Almighty!

The Holy Quran, refers to the Jews who serve God in this Name as "Yahood' or power-brokers. (Jehovah, God Almighty, Seekers of power) in their service to God. English is a language designed to accommodate abridgement, seen in the coming and the going, illustrated by the age-old question, "Is man standing still with time passing him by, or is time standing still and man is passing through it?" Arabic and Hebrew are both Semitic languages that speak profoundly to the coming and the going.

He left the job with us.

Appendix:

- *Wisdom from Grandfather to Grandson*

- *Paintings by Author*

- *Photographs*

Some of the many insights of wisdom, quoted by my most beloved grandfather, the honorable Elijah Muhammad:

"Son, when you catch-a-hold to the Gospel-plow, there is no turning back (He himself, the son of a Southern Baptist Preacher)".

"Son, I never said there was nothing beyond the Sun, Moon, and Stars, only that our business is here".

"Son, man's life before Allah is but as a flickering of a candle in the night; we're gone before we even realize we're here good."

"If you find someone digging a hole for you, you wait until its good and deep and then you push them off in it."

"Son, those women went after me (afflicted with the woes of a polygamous life, in a western culture)!"

"No one wanted to awaken the sleeping lion, for fear they maybe his first meal (a potential seen in our people)."

Oil by Jesus Muhammad-Ali

1969, Oil by Jesus Muhammad-Ali

Just a few of the Grandsons and Granddaughters of Sister Clara and the Hon. Elijah Muhammad

Muhammad Ali meets President Ronald Reagan

Islam's three Sacred Precincts: Mecca, Jerusalem, and Medina